This is Mars.

Image credit: NASA/JPL-Caltech

Image credit: NASA/JPL/Texas A&M/Cornell

Mars is far away from Earth.
The Sun looks small on Mars.

Mars is dry.
There are no lakes or rivers.
There are no oceans.
There is no rain.

Is there water on Mars? Let's find out!

Image credit: NASA/JPL-Caltech/MSSS

Image credits: (left) NASA/JPL-Caltech/MSSS, (above) NASA

Mars is not a good place for people.
The air is not good to breathe.
We can send robots to Mars.
Robots can do work on Mars for people.
Robots do not need air or food or water.

Image credit: NASA

How do robots get to Mars?
They fly in a rocket ship. It is a six month trip.

Mariner 9 was an orbiter.
It flew around Mars.
It took these pictures of Mars.

Image credit: NASA/JPL

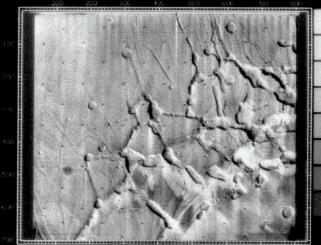

Image credits: NASA Goddard

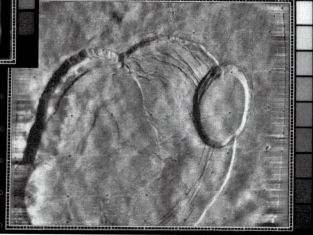

1971-1972

Viking 1 was the first lander. It landed on Mars.

Image credit: NASA/JPL-Caltech/University of Arizona

Viking 2 also landed on Mars. It took this picture.

Image credit: NASA Ames Research Center

The Viking landers studied the air and the rocks.
But they could not move. They could not drive to new rocks.

Image credit: NASA/JPL

1976-1982

Mars Global Surveyor orbited Mars for 9 years.

It looked at dust storms. It made maps. It looked for good places to land.

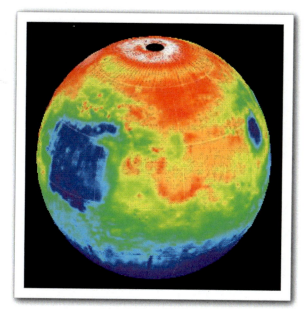

It made this map of the kinds of rocks on Mars.

It took pictures of Mars.

Image credits: (left) NASA/JPL-Caltech
(above) NASA/JPL/ASU
(right) NASA/JPL/Malin Space Science Systems

1997-2006

Mars Pathfinder had a lander and a rover.

The rover was named Sojourner. The lander was named Sagan.

Air bags helped them land.

Then Sojourner rolled off to look around.

Image credits: (above) NASA, (left) NASA/JPL

Sojourner was the first rover to drive on Mars.

Image credits: (above) NASA/JPL, (right) NASA

Sagan took this picture. Can you see Sojourner?

1997

Image credits: (above) NASA, (right) NASA/JPL, (facing) NASA/JPL

Here are the pictures that Sojourner sent to Earth.

Mars Odyssey has been at Mars for 17 years!
It helps rovers talk to people on Earth.
It found ice on Mars.

2001-?

Image credits: NASA/Kennedy Space Center

Spirit and Opportunity are twin rovers.
They took off to Mars in 2003.

Each rover landed with a parachute and airbags.
Then the lander opened up, and the rover was ready to go.

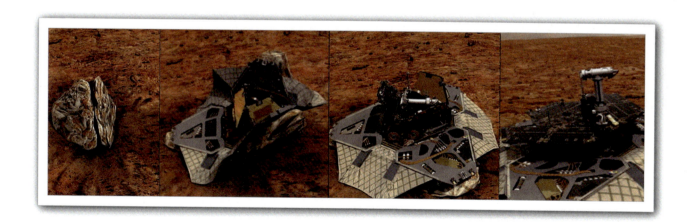

Image credits: NASA/JPL

2003-2010 2003-?

Spirit and Opportunity have an arm with tools.
They can drill rocks.

Opportunity made this hole in a rock to see what was inside.

Image credit: NASA/JPL-Caltech/Cornell

Image credit: NASA/JPL

Image credit: NASA/JPL/Cornell/USGS

Spirit and Opportunity saw that Mars once had water. The rocks show that Mars was once wet.

Image credit: NASA/JPL-Caltech/Cornell

Spirit and Opportunity get energy from the sun.
They have solar panels.
Opportunity is still working on Mars.

Image credit: NASA/JPL-Caltech/Cornell

Spirit does not work now. It is stuck in sand.
It has too much dust on its solar panels.
No one is on Mars to brush it off.
But Spirit is not sad. Spirit is a robot.

The Mars Reconnaissance Orbiter takes pictures of Mars.

Image credits: NASA/JPL-Caltech/Univ. of Arizona (above), JPL/NASA (facing)

2006-?

Image credit: NASA/JPL/UA/Lockheed Martin

The Phoenix lander went to the North Pole of Mars to test the dirt and ice.
It was not a rover. It had no wheels.
It used solar panels for energy.

The Phoenix lander used a scoop to pick up dirt.

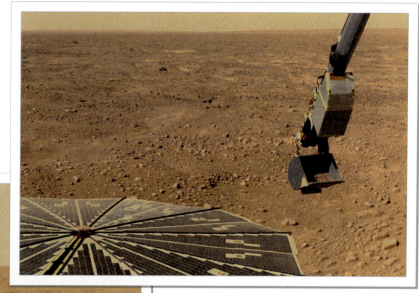

Image credits: NASA/JPL-Caltech/University of Arizona/Texas A&M University

2008

This is Curiosity.

It is the biggest robot to go to Mars.
Curiosity is as big as a car.

It does not have solar panels. It uses nuclear power. Dust does not stop it.

Curiosity can do many tests on rocks.

NASA/JPL-Caltech/MSSS

2012-?

Image Credits: NASA/JPL-Caltech

Curiosity was too big to use airbags to land.
First it used a parachute. Then it used a sky crane.

Curiosity can drive all day.
It does not get tired.
It does not get bored.

NASA/JPL-Caltech

Image Credit: NASA/JPL-Caltech/MSSS

Curiosity has many tools.
It learns about air, water, and rocks on Mars.

Image credit: NASA Goddard

Maybe one day you will go to Mars.
Or maybe will you help build a rover.
There is still so much to learn.

This is not Mars! This silly picture is on Earth.
The rovers did not meet on Mars.
They were not in the same place.

Image Credit (left): NASA, ESA, the Hubble Heritage Team (STScI/AURA), J. Bell (ASU), and M. Wolff (Space Science Institute) , (above) NASA/JPL-Caltech

Coming soon!

All text copyright © 2018 Catherine Sarisky. All images are courtesy of NASA and its partners, as noted. Image credit (this page): NASA/JPL-CALTECH, (cover) NASA/JPL-Caltech/MSSS

Made in the USA
Middletown, DE
02 June 2018